# ENGINEER
· ⊗ · ⊗ · ⊗ · ⊗ · ⊗ · ⊗ · ⊗ · ⊗ ·
# ACADEMY

First American Edition 2017
Kane Miller, A Division of EDC Publishing

Copyright © 2017 Quarto Publishing plc

Published by arrangement with Ivy Kids, an imprint of The Quarto Group.

For information contact:
Kane Miller, A Division of EDC Publishing
PO Box 470663
Tulsa, OK 74147-0663
**www.kanemiller.com**
**www.edcpub.com**
**www.usbornebooksandmore.com**

Library of Congress Control Number: 2016934250

Printed in China

ISBN: 978-1-61067-546-8

4 5 6 7 8 9 10

# ENGINEER
## ACADEMY

WRITTEN BY
**STEVE MARTIN**

ILLUSTRATED BY
**NASTIA SLEPTSOVA**

**Kane Miller**
A DIVISION OF EDC PUBLISHING

# CONTENTS

## ENERGY ENGINEER

## ALTERNATIVE ENERGY ENGINEER

## MATERIALS ENGINEER

## ENGINEER'S TOOLBOX

# WELCOME TO ENGINEER ACADEMY!

Engineers use their skills and knowledge to design, make, repair and look after engines, energy systems, machines, robots and all kinds of important things.

Try to imagine what life would be like without these people. You would sit at home in the dark and cold because there would be no lights or heating. You wouldn't have much to do because there would be no computers, no telephones and no television. And, if you decided to go out, you wouldn't go far because there wouldn't be any cars or buses.

As you'll find out, our world depends on engineers. However, engineering isn't just important for how it helps us. Being an engineer is one of the most exciting and interesting jobs anyone can have.

**So, good job on joining Engineer Academy.
You've made a great decision.**

**Before you start, you must register at the Academy. Fill in your details on the Trainee Engineer Card.**

## TRAINEE ENGINEER

FIRST NAME:

LAST NAME:

AGE:

DATE JOINED:

To graduate from Engineer Academy, you must complete the tasks in this book and earn all your task stickers and qualification certificates.

# MEET THE
# ENGINEERS

It can be surprising to learn that there are so many types of engineering jobs. Planning a coal mine uses different skills from building a robot or designing an airplane. At Engineer Academy, you will qualify in different branches of engineering. This will help you to decide what type of engineer you want to be.

## MECHANICAL ENGINEERS
can be experts with all kinds of machines. They might have jobs looking after machinery, or they may invent new machines to carry out different tasks.

## AEROSPACE ENGINEERS
design, build and look after airplanes. Some aerospace engineers even work on spacecraft and satellites.

## ROBOTICS ENGINEERS

create robots and think up new ways of using them to work for us.

## ENERGY ENGINEERS

work with different power sources to produce energy for our homes, schools, factories and offices. They might work in coal mines, or with gas, oil or nuclear power.

## ALTERNATIVE ENERGY ENGINEERS help us to

capture energy from sources such as the wind, sea, rivers and the sun.

## MATERIALS ENGINEERS

study metals, plastics and other materials and discover new ways to use them. They also invent new materials: for example, by mixing different metals together.

# MACHINES:LEVERS

Mechanical engineers work with machines. A machine is a device that makes work easier. It does this by increasing the effect of our efforts. One of the simplest machines is the lever. By using a lever, you can lift heavy weights with less effort.

A seesaw is a type of lever. Look at these pictures. The two boys are heavier than the girl, so they move down. But when the boys move closer to the balancing point in the center (called the "fulcrum"), the boys and the girl are balanced. Because the girl is farther from the fulcrum, she can lift a weight much heavier than herself.

We use levers in a lot of places, including some that aren't that obvious!

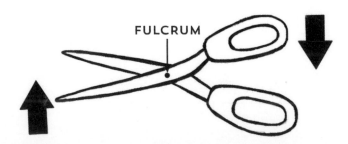

FULCRUM

## EXPERIMENT WITH LEVERS

**You will be examining how a light weight can lift and balance heavier weights when we move the fulcrum.**

**You will need:** a ruler, something to balance it on (a hardback book is perfect), 9 pennies

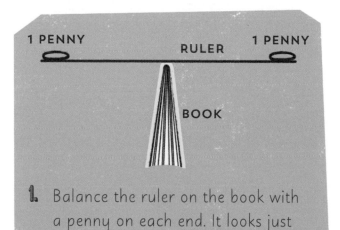

1 PENNY          RULER          1 PENNY

BOOK

**1.** Balance the ruler on the book with a penny on each end. It looks just like a seesaw.

2 PENNIES          RULER          1 PENNY

BOOK

**2.** Now put two pennies on one end and slide the ruler along until it balances. Make a note of where the top of the book is, using the inch marks on the ruler. Write this measurement down in the table.

**3.** Do the same with four, six and eight pennies.

| | DISTANCE (INCHES) |
|---|---|
| 2 PENNIES | |
| 4 PENNIES | |
| 6 PENNIES | |
| 8 PENNIES | |

**Once you have completed the table, place your sticker here.**

**PLACE STICKER HERE**

⊘ TASK COMPLETE ⊘

# MACHINES:
## PULLEYS

A pulley is a machine that uses ropes and wheels to make weights easier to lift. A simple pulley works like this: a rope runs through a groove in a wheel. It has a load on one end and someone pulling on the other. As the person pulls down on the rope, the load goes up. It's easier to pull **DOWN** on the rope than to lift the load **UP** yourself because you are working with the force of gravity (the force that pulls things downward), not against it.

The really smart thing about pulleys is this: if you arrange the pulleys in a certain way, then the more pulleys you use, the easier it becomes to lift a load. With two pulleys instead of one, the amount of effort needed to lift the load is half as much. With four pulleys, the effort is halved again. The more pulleys you add, the farther you need to pull the rope, but it becomes much easier to pull.

PULLEY

EFFORT

LOAD

WITH ENOUGH PULLEYS, YOU CAN LIFT AN ELEPHANT!

# MAKE A SIMPLE PULLEY

**You will need:** twine, scissors, an empty thread spool, adhesive tape, a weight to lift (for example, a toy)

**1.** Thread the twine through the ends of the thread spool.

**2.** Tape or tie each end of the twine to the back of a chair. Move the chairs apart until the string is quite taut.

**3.** Tie another length of string to the weight. Place the weight on the floor and loop the twine over the thread spool.

**4.** You are now ready to use your pulley to raise and lower the weight.

**Once you have made your pulley, place your sticker here.**

PLACE STICKER HERE

# MAKING THE WHEELS TURN

Automotive engineers design and build engine-powered land vehicles, such as cars, buses and trucks, all of which depend on the greatest engineering invention of all time— the **WHEEL**!

Wheels usually turn around a rod, known as an axle. One axle joins a car's front wheels together, while another joins the back wheels.

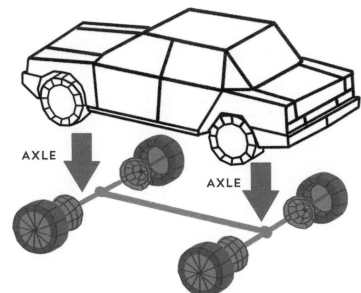

AXLE

AXLE

## DESIGN A CAR

**You will need:** a small rectangular cardboard box, a pen, a jar, thick cardboard, two pencils, a pair of scissors, an adult helper

1. Draw two lines, A and B, across the bottom of the box, to divide it into three equal sections. Next, draw a rectangle in the middle section, leaving a border of about .5 inches around it.

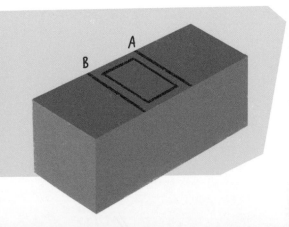

**2.** With an adult's help, cut along the lines shown in green.

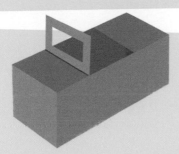

**3.** Fold along the red line. You have now made the hood, windshield and trunk.

**4.** Draw around a jar to make four circles on the cardboard and cut them out.

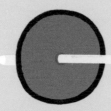

**5.** Draw a thick black line around the edges of the circles to turn them into tires. With an adult's help, make a hole in the center of each circle with the point of a pencil.

**6.** Push a pencil through the front of the box, from one side to the other. Make sure it's at the right height for the wheel to turn. Do the same at the back.

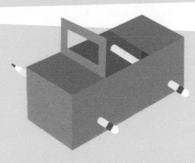

**7.** Attach the wheels to the axles. Your vehicle is now ready for testing!

**When you have completed your car, place your sticker here.**

**PLACE STICKER HERE**

# GEARS

Cars, trucks and other vehicles, including bicycles, use gears.
The gears on a bicycle are there to make cycling easier.

A gear is made up of two cogs of different sizes joined together.
A cog is simply a wheel with teeth.

## HOW DOES A BICYCLE WORK?

On a bicycle, the cogs are connected by a chain.
On this gear, the front cog, where you pedal, has
twice as many teeth as the cog at the back wheel.
This means every time you pedal one turn, the
front cog moves around once, but the back
cog moves around twice. This makes the back wheel
move around twice, too, which helps you go faster.

## BIGGER BACK COG

The bigger the cog at the back (with more
teeth), the slower it turns, but the more
force it has. This makes big cogs helpful
when you are pedaling uphill.

## SMALLER BACK COG

The smaller the cog at the back (with
fewer teeth), the faster it turns. This
makes small cogs useful if you want to
move quickly, such as when you are
cycling down a slope.

# TEST YOUR COG KNOWLEDGE

Look at these gears and work out how many times the back wheel cog will turn for one turn of the pedal. You will need to divide the number of teeth on the pedal cog by the number of teeth on the back cog. Check your answers below.

**A.**

BACK
WHEEL
COG

PEDAL
COG

_____ turns

**B.**

_____ turns

**C.**

_____ turns

Once you have worked out the number of turns for each gear, place your sticker here.

**PLACE STICKER HERE**

ANSWERS: A. 2, B. 3, C. 4

⊘ **TASK COMPLETE** ⊘

# ENGINES

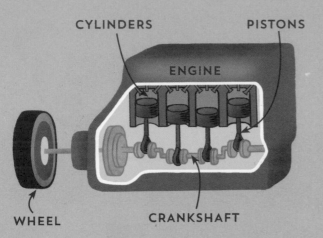

**CYLINDERS**  **PISTONS**

**ENGINE**

**WHEEL**  **CRANKSHAFT**

The most important part of a car is the engine. It produces the power that turns the wheels. The engine has a number of cylinders, or tubes (most cars have four). Inside each is a piston, which moves up and down. The pistons are connected to a shaft known as a crankshaft. This changes the up-and-down movement of the pistons into an around-and-around movement, which turns the wheels!

**i**

**ENGINEER INFO**

Each of the pistons moves in four stages:

**AIR & FUEL**

**1.** The piston moves down, sucking air and fuel into the cylinder.

**2.** The piston moves up, squashing the air and fuel.

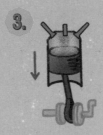

**3.** A spark explodes the air and fuel mixture, forcing the piston down.

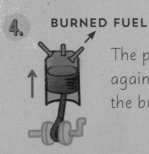

**4.** **BURNED FUEL**

The piston moves up again, pushing out the burned fuel.

**CONGRATULATIONS!** You have now qualified as a mechanical engineer. Fill in the details on the certificate below.

## ——— QUALIFIED ———
# MECHANICAL ENGINEER

**ENGINEER NAME:**

The above-named engineer
has learned about levers, pulleys,
wheels, axles, gears and engines
and is now fully qualified in

## MECHANICAL ENGINEERING.

**QUALIFICATION DATE:**

# AIRFLOW

Aerospace engineers design and build airplanes. You will be building and comparing your own airplanes, but first, let's look at an important part of aircraft design—**AERODYNAMICS**. This might sound complicated, but all it means is how air moves around an object.

### HOW DOES A PLANE WORK?

A plane's engines push it forward, but air resistance slows it down. This is why airplanes have a narrow shape—there is less surface for the air to hit. Airplane wings have a special shape that moves the air in a way that helps the plane lift into the air.

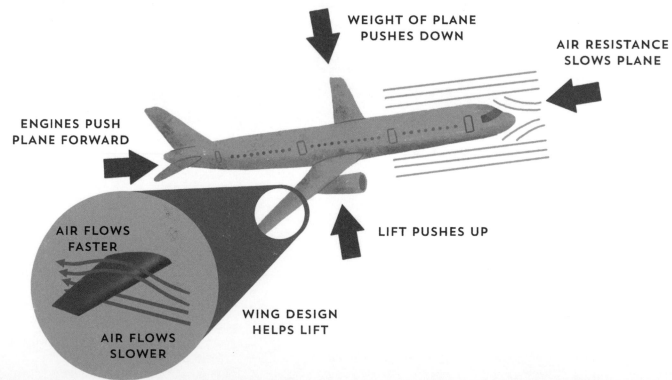

WEIGHT OF PLANE
PUSHES DOWN

AIR RESISTANCE
SLOWS PLANE

ENGINES PUSH
PLANE FORWARD

LIFT PUSHES UP

AIR FLOWS
FASTER

WING DESIGN
HELPS LIFT

AIR FLOWS
SLOWER

## BUILD A PLANE: THE DART

**You will need:** a letter-size piece of paper

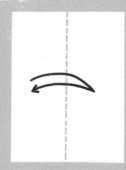

**1.** Fold the piece of paper in half lengthwise, to make a crease. Then flatten it out again.

**2.** Fold down the two top corners so they meet at the crease in the center.

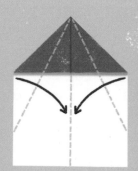

**3.** Fold the two edges toward the crease in the center, as shown.

**4.** Fold the plane in half along the crease.

**5.** Turn the plane on its side. Fold down each wing along the crease, as shown.

**6.** Fold up the wing edges. Your aerodynamic plane is now ready to fly! Its narrow shape means there is less air resistance, so it can fly quickly.

**Keep your plane safe—you will need it for the challenge on the next page.**

**Once you have made your plane, place your sticker here.**

**PLACE STICKER HERE**

✎ **TASK COMPLETE** ✎

# FLIGHT OF THE CONDOR

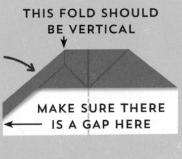

## BUILD A PLANE: THE CONDOR

**The Condor is a different kind of plane compared to the Dart. It has a wider, flatter shape. After you build it, you will be carrying out test flights to compare your two airplanes.**

**You will need:** a letter-size piece of paper

**1.** Take the piece of paper and turn it sideways, so the long sides are at the top and bottom. Fold it so there is a crease down the center and then open it up again.

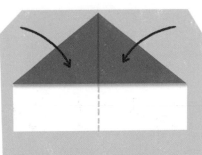

**2.** Fold the two top corners so that they meet in the center.

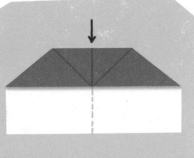

**3.** Fold the nose down so that it meets at the line, as shown.

**THIS FOLD SHOULD BE VERTICAL**

**MAKE SURE THERE IS A GAP HERE**

**4.** Fold the left edge over, as shown. The fold should be about .75 inches wide.

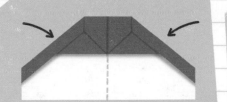

**5.** Do the same on the other side.

**6.** Now fold the plane in half.

**7.** Fold down the wings, as shown.

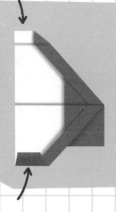

**8.** Fold up the edges of the wings slightly—about .75 inches. The Condor is now ready to launch!

**Now that you have made the two planes, fly them both and mark which plane came out best on each of the following tests:**

| | THE DART | THE CONDOR |
|---|---|---|
| WHICH PLANE FLEW THE FARTHEST? | | |
| WHICH PLANE FLEW THE FASTEST? | | |
| WHICH PLANE WAS IN THE AIR THE LONGEST? | | |

**The answers to your test flights should help you to see why fighter jets are so slim, and why gliders have such long wingspans.**

**Once you have completed your test flights, place your sticker here.**

**PLACE STICKER HERE**

⌘ TASK COMPLETE ⌘

# JET ENGINES

A jet engine on an airplane works by burning fuel, which forces energy to shoot out of the back of it. Whichever direction the gas moves, the plane moves in the opposite direction.

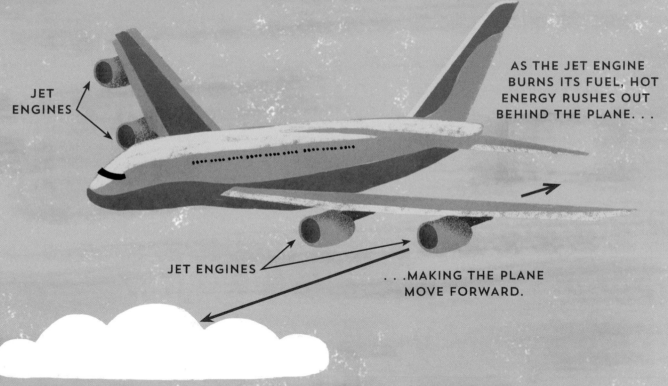

JET ENGINES

AS THE JET ENGINE BURNS ITS FUEL, HOT ENERGY RUSHES OUT BEHIND THE PLANE. . .

JET ENGINES

. . .MAKING THE PLANE MOVE FORWARD.

## MAKE YOUR OWN JET ENGINE

**To show how the engines on an airplane work, you can make your own balloon jet engine.**

**You will need:** *a balloon, a bendable straw, a rubber band, an adult helper*

**1.** Blow up the balloon and ask an adult to hold the end tightly so that the air does not escape.

**2.** Slide a straw through the adult's fingers into the balloon. They will need to keep pressing tightly. If any air escapes, you can blow up the balloon again with the straw inside.

**3.** Carefully tie a rubber band tightly around the mouth of the balloon to keep the straw in place.

**4.** Still holding the mouth of the balloon tightly, place the balloon on the floor with the straw straight. Let go and watch what happens! The air will rush out and force the balloon to move forward.

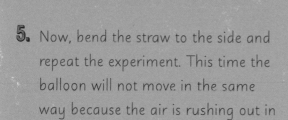

**5.** Now, bend the straw to the side and repeat the experiment. This time the balloon will not move in the same way because the air is rushing out in a different direction.

**Once you have tested your balloon jet engine, place your sticker here.**

**PLACE STICKER HERE**

⊘ **TASK COMPLETE** ⊘

AEROSPACE
ENGINEER

# BLASTOFF!

There is a special type of aerospace engineering known as astronautics engineering. It involves designing and testing machines for use in space. Imagine how much work goes into designing a spacecraft that has to travel at thousands of miles an hour, cope with extreme temperatures and survive being hit by fast-moving space particles!

### ROCKETS
take astronauts or satellites into space.

### SPACE STATIONS
provide a home for astronauts orbiting Earth.

**SATELLITES** orbit Earth. They are used for communications and forecasting the weather.

**PROBES** are sent off to explore our solar system.

ENGINEER
INFO

**SPACE BUGGIES** allow astronauts to travel around on the moon.

**CONGRATULATIONS!** You have now qualified as an aerospace engineer. Fill in the details on the certificate below.

# — QUALIFIED —
# AEROSPACE ENGINEER

**ENGINEER NAME:**

The above-named engineer
has learned about aerodynamics,
jet engines and astronautics engineering
and is now fully qualified in

## AEROSPACE ENGINEERING.

**QUALIFICATION DATE:**

# ROBOTS

Robotics engineers work with robots. A robot is a machine designed to do work that we can't or don't want to do. For example, robots can explore the dangerous surface of Mars, or they can stand on a factory production line doing the job of putting the tops on bottles.

**LABEL THE ROBOT PARTS**

**Imagine that you are a robot. Which parts of your body would be the control, the machine and the sensors? Label the picture and then check your answers at the bottom of page 29.**

Robots usually have three main parts. These are:

**THE CONTROL** The part that tells the robot what to do—usually a computer.

**THE MACHINE** The parts of the robot that can make, repair and move things.

**THE SENSORS** The parts that tell the robot about the outside world, such as where an object is.

Your brain would be the
_____

Your eyes and ears would be the
_____

Your arms and legs would be the
_____

## DESIGN THE ULTIMATE ROBOT!

Draw the ultimate robot below. First, decide what you want it to do: play games with you, do your homework, make popcorn and so on. Then think about what it will need to do these jobs—detachable tennis racquet arms, a super-computer brain, a popcorn-maker stomach? Make sure it has a control, moving machine parts and a sensor.

**Once you have designed your robot, place your sticker here.**

PLACE STICKER HERE

⊘ TASK COMPLETE ⊘

# A HELPING HAND

Most robots are used in factories where the same items are made over and over again. Robots are faster than people, probably won't make mistakes and don't need rest breaks.

Robots are particularly important in car manufacturing. When a car is being made, it moves along a production line, where different robot arms carry out different tasks. Of course, robots can't actually design the car—we need human engineers for that.

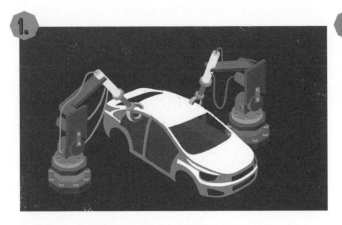

**ASSEMBLING:** Robots piece the car body together.

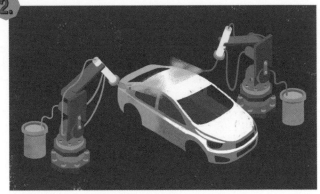

**PAINTING:** Robots spray the car with paint.

**FINAL TASKS:** People finish putting the car together.

The robot arms doing the assembling and painting on the production line are the "machine" part of the robot. The design of the mechanical arms depends on what job the robot is needed to do.

## MAKE A MECHANICAL GRABBER ARM

**You are going to make your own mechanical arm! It will be used for picking things up.**

**You will need:** two 6-inch rulers, two rubber bands, a letter-size piece of paper

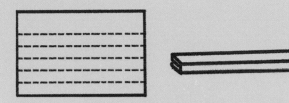

**1.** Take the piece of paper and fold it over and over lengthwise until it is a strip about 1.5 inches wide.

**2.** Roll up the strip of paper and place it between two rulers, about 1.5 inches from the end.

**3.** Wrap two rubber bands over the rulers, one on each side of the rolled-up paper.

**4.** Your mechanical arm is ready! Position the arm over the object you want to pick up, and press down on the paper to grasp it.

**Don't worry if you can't find two rulers. You can use sticks, pens or anything that is fairly long and thin. You could even use chopsticks and then practice eating with them! (You will need to alter the size of the paper to fit what you use.)**

**Once you have built and tested your grabber, place your sticker here.**

**PLACE STICKER HERE**

**TASK COMPLETE**

31

# SENSORS

Robots have different types of sensors.

## VISION SENSORS

The Mars Curiosity Rover robot explores the planet Mars. It uses cameras connected to a computer to make decisions about which way to go. It is important that the Rover can steer itself because of the time delay in sending images from Mars to Earth. By the time the controllers on Earth see the pictures, the robot could have fallen off a cliff.

## HEAT SENSORS

The Mars Rover has a sensor that measures the planet's temperature, as well as sensors that record a lot of other useful information, such as wind speed, radiation and the amount of liquid in the air.

## SOUND SENSORS

If a robot has sound sensors, it can be programmed to respond to commands. For example, a toy robot might start walking when it hears a clap and stop when it hears another one.

## TOUCH SENSORS

Touch sensors allow robots to apply different amounts of force to an object. A robot in a factory needs to grip metal objects firmly while using a lighter touch on materials such as glass.

ENGINEER
INFO

**CONGRATULATIONS!** You have now qualified
as a robotics engineer. Fill in the details on the certificate below.

# — QUALIFIED —
# ROBOTICS ENGINEER

**ENGINEER NAME:**

The above-named engineer has
learned about robot controls,
machine parts and sensors
and is now fully qualified in

## ROBOTICS ENGINEERING.

**QUALIFICATION DATE:**

# ELECTRICITY
## —IN THE HOME—

Electricity is one of the most important types of energy we have. There are two ways we power things with electricity. The first is to use batteries. These are usually used for smaller items we carry around, such as mobile phones, toys and TV remote controls. The second way we power things is to plug them into an outlet that is connected to the electrical circuit in a building.

**WIRES** run behind the walls and under the floor and lead to sockets.

**ELECTRICITY SUPPLY**
enters the home through above-ground or underground wires.

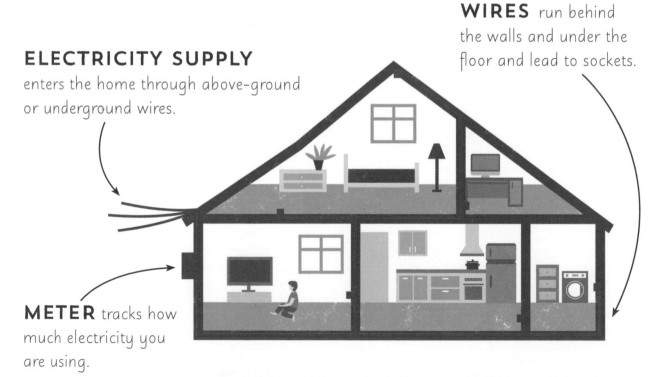

**METER** tracks how much electricity you are using.

Because electricity is so powerful, it is extremely dangerous. If electricity runs through a person's body, it is called electrocution. You must make sure this NEVER happens because it can be deadly.

## LEARN ABOUT THE DANGERS OF ELECTRICITY

There are six dangerous situations in the picture below. Draw a circle around each one. You can check your answers on page 64.

Once you have found all of the dangers, place your sticker here.

**PLACE STICKER HERE**

◙ TASK COMPLETE ◙

# ELECTRICAL —CIRCUITS—

Electricity can come from batteries or from an outlet in the wall, but in both cases, the electrical device using the power has to be linked to the source of the electricity.

Electricity runs through wires. These are usually made of copper because electricity moves through this metal easily. The wire is covered in plastic to prevent people from touching the copper and electrocuting themselves.

There is a special name for a power source connected to an electrical device with wires. It is called an electrical circuit. A circuit has to be a closed loop or else it will not work. This is how a switch—such as a light switch—works.

**TURNING A LIGHT ON:** the switch closes the circuit so that electricity can move through it and power the light.

**TURNING A LIGHT OFF:** the switch opens and breaks the circuit. This stops the flow of electricity to the light and turns it off.

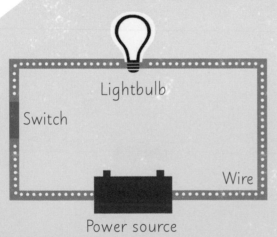

Lightbulb

Switch

Wire

Power source

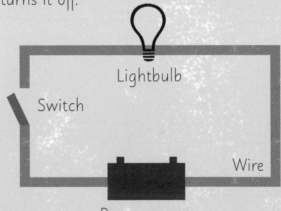

Lightbulb

Switch

Wire

Power source

# TEST YOUR ELECTRICAL ENGINEERING SKILLS

Decide which two of the four circuits below would light up the bulb, then color those two lightbulbs yellow. Remember, a circuit needs to be closed for the light to come on. You can check your answers at the bottom of the page.

A.

B.

C.

D.

When you have figured out which two circuits work, place your sticker here.

**PLACE STICKER HERE**

# —POWER—
# STATIONS

Most of the electricity in your home is produced in a power station and sent to your home through cables (bundles of wires). Different types of power stations use different types of fuel, including coal, gas and oil. In some, the power of wind or water is used instead. But they all make electricity in the same way—by turning the blades of a big fan called a **TURBINE**, which drives a **GENERATOR**, which makes electricity.

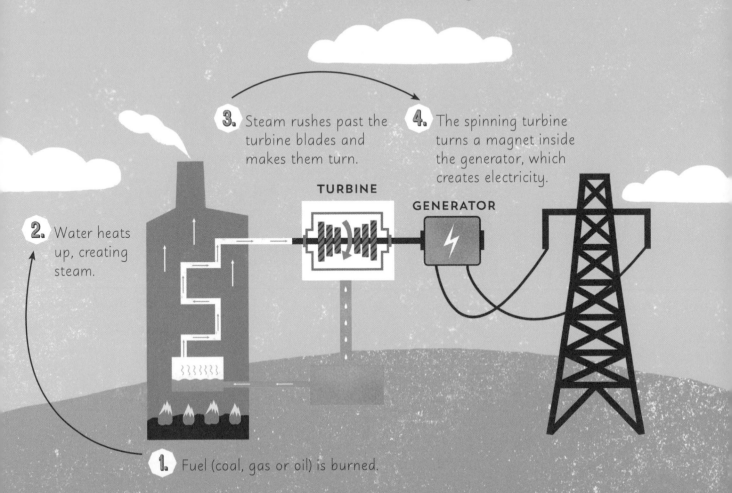

**3.** Steam rushes past the turbine blades and makes them turn.

**4.** The spinning turbine turns a magnet inside the generator, which creates electricity.

**TURBINE**

**GENERATOR**

**2.** Water heats up, creating steam.

**1.** Fuel (coal, gas or oil) is burned.

# WHAT IS ELECTRICITY?

Everything is made of atoms—they are the tiny building blocks for everything in the universe. Atoms are made up of even smaller particles, including electrons, which spin around the center (nucleus) of an atom. Electricity is simply the movement of electrons from one atom to another.

A generator works by spinning a magnet inside a wire. This makes the electrons in the wire move, which creates electricity.

ATOM

NUCLEUS

ELECTRONS

## RENEWABLE OR NOT?

**Some types of fuel get used up and cannot be replaced. Others can be used again and again—these are called renewable energy sources. Which of the energy sources on the right are renewable, and which are not? Circle the correct answer.**

| | | |
|---|---|---|
| COAL | RENEWABLE | NONRENEWABLE |
| WIND | RENEWABLE | NONRENEWABLE |
| GAS | RENEWABLE | NONRENEWABLE |
| WATER | RENEWABLE | NONRENEWABLE |
| OIL | RENEWABLE | NONRENEWABLE |

**Once you have checked your answers below, place your sticker here.**

**PLACE STICKER HERE**

ANSWERS: Coal - nonrenewable, Wind - renewable, Gas - nonrenewable, Water - renewable, Oil - nonrenewable

⊘ **TASK COMPLETE** ⊘

ENERGY ENGINEER

# ELECTRICITY
## — AT A TOUCH —

## POWER JOURNEY

**Use the stickers at the back of the book to complete the journey of electricity, starting at the coal mine and ending at the TV. There are seven stickers in total.**

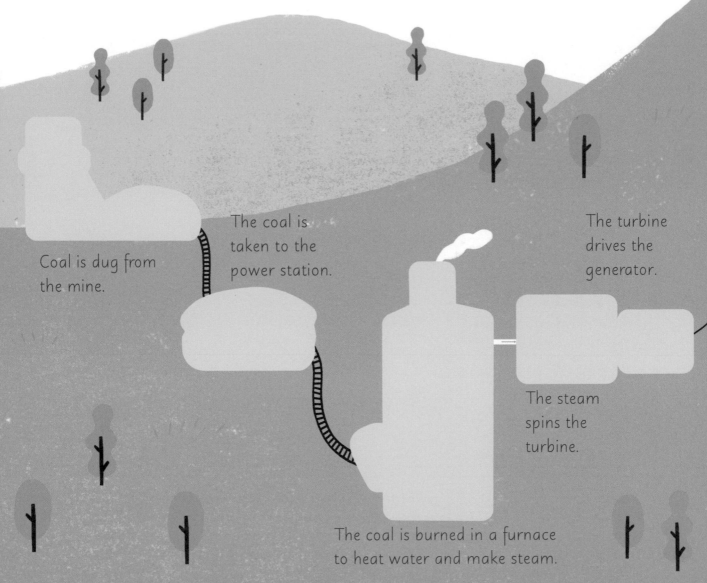

Coal is dug from the mine.

The coal is taken to the power station.

The turbine drives the generator.

The steam spins the turbine.

The coal is burned in a furnace to heat water and make steam.

Electricity enters the house.

Power lines carry the electricity.

The child turns on the TV, which is plugged into the home's electrical circuit. Electricity flows into it, and a TV program appears!

Once you have completed the journey from coal mine to TV, place your sticker here.

**PLACE STICKER HERE**

**TASK COMPLETE**

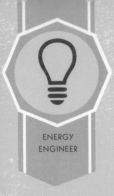

# MINING

As you saw on the previous page, the first step of producing energy is finding a source of fuel. For power stations that run on coal, this means digging the coal out of the earth.

Mining engineers help to design coal mines, and then make sure that they are run safely and efficiently. This is a difficult job because mines can be hundreds of feet below ground. The tunnels can be so long that miners have to get to the coal face (the place where the coal is dug out) on a train.

If that isn't hard enough, the mining engineer also has to make sure that there are no rock collapses, and that the mine does not flood. There are also risks from dangerous underground gases that can cause fire or explosions.

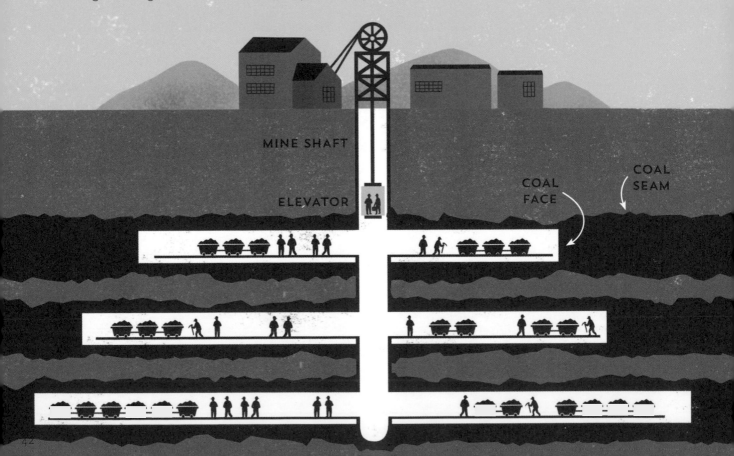

MINE SHAFT

ELEVATOR

COAL FACE

COAL SEAM

## PRACTICE YOUR PROBLEM-SOLVING

Engineers need to be good at solving problems. To practice your skills, see if you can help the miner find his way to the coal face, avoiding the dangerous mine collapses, floods and gas leaks along the way.

Once you have completed the maze, place your sticker here.

PLACE STICKER HERE

⬤ TASK COMPLETE ⬤

# NUCLEAR —POWER—

Some power stations use nuclear power to make electricity. A machine known as a nuclear reactor splits apart the atoms of a metal called uranium into smaller atoms. Once the first atom is split, it flies off in parts, and these parts split other atoms, which fly off and split other atoms, which…well, you get the idea. This is called a **CHAIN REACTION**. It's a bit like knocking over a row of dominoes, or firing a marble into a group of marbles, which then crash into other marbles. But in a nuclear reactor, the chain reaction keeps going!

Splitting apart uranium atoms releases huge amounts of energy, which is used to heat water and produce steam. The steam drives a turbine, which turns a generator to produce electricity.

Nuclear engineers make sure that nuclear power stations are safe, and that dangerous radioactive waste is gotten rid of safely.

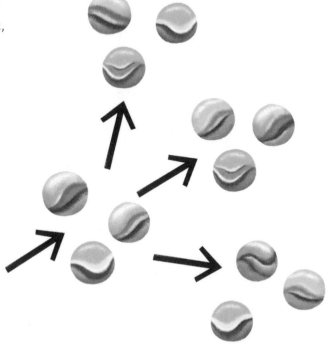

ENGINEER
INFO

44

# CONGRATULATIONS! You have now qualified
as an energy engineer. Fill in the details on the certificate below.

## — QUALIFIED —
## ENERGY ENGINEER

**ENGINEER NAME:**

The above-named engineer has
learned about electricity, circuits, turbines,
generators, power stations, coal mines and
nuclear power and is now fully qualified in

## ENERGY ENGINEERING.

**QUALIFICATION DATE:**

# WINDMILLS

Alternative energy engineers work with renewable energy. This is energy that comes from sources that do not get used up and run out. However much wind, wave or river flow you use, there will always be more.

This does not mean that these renewable energy sources have just been invented. Believe it or not, wind was a great help to our ancestors when they were making bread. The wind was used by windmills to grind grain into flour—the main ingredient in bread.

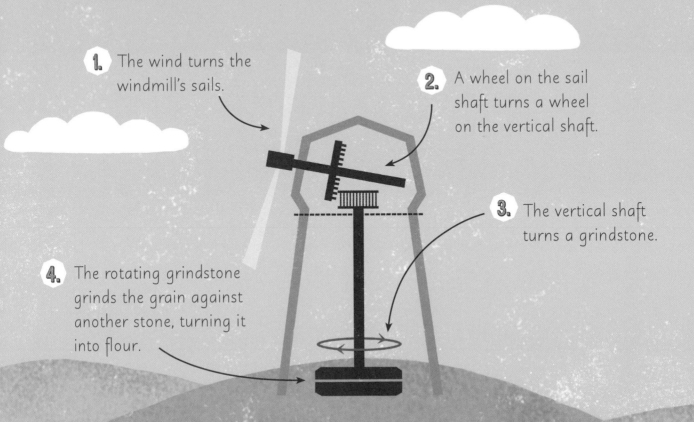

**1.** The wind turns the windmill's sails.

**2.** A wheel on the sail shaft turns a wheel on the vertical shaft.

**3.** The vertical shaft turns a grindstone.

**4.** The rotating grindstone grinds the grain against another stone, turning it into flour.

# MAKE A WIND TURBINE

On the cover flaps of this book, there is a press-out model of a wind turbine. Pop out the pieces, then fold down along the dashed lines. Follow the instructions to construct your model.

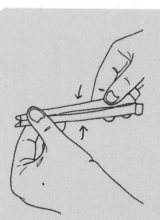

**1.** Glue tab 1 to tab 1 and so on, until you reach tab 6.

**2.** To make the Head, glue tab 6 to tab 6. Fold each end inward and slot together, making a rectangular slanted box.

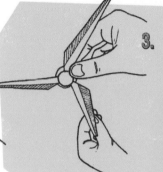

**3.** Attach the Blades to the Hub back by sticking the matching numbered tabs together. Glue the Hub front to the Hub back; the Blades will be between them.

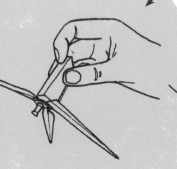

**4.** With the help of an adult, pierce the center of the Hub and Blades with a thumbtack and then fix it to the Head as shown. Your Blades should spin!

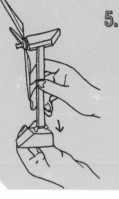

**5.** Finally, piece together your wind turbine. Slot the top of the Pole into the bottom of the Head. Slot the bottom of the Pole into the Base, securing the tabs with glue.

Once you have built your wind turbine, place your sticker here.

**PLACE STICKER HERE**

⦿ TASK COMPLETE ⦿

# WATER POWER: WATERWHEELS

People have been using the power of water for thousands of years. Waterwheels were once placed in fast-flowing streams that turned the wheel. This moved other parts of machinery, which were used for everything from grinding grain to hammering iron or crushing rocks.

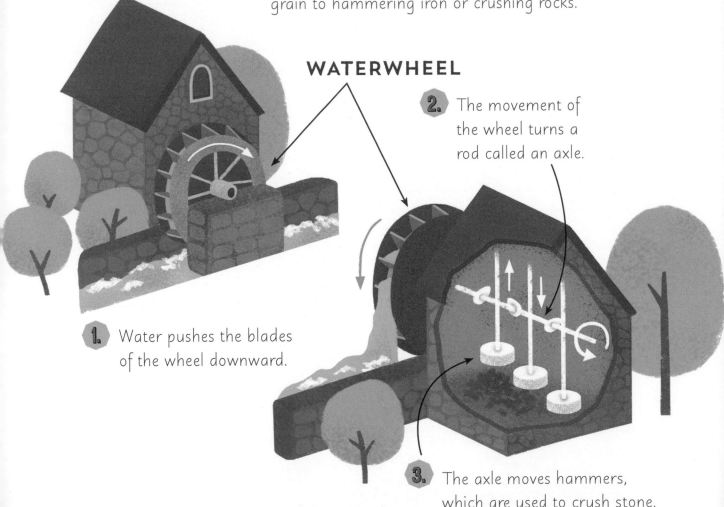

**WATERWHEEL**

**2.** The movement of the wheel turns a rod called an axle.

**1.** Water pushes the blades of the wheel downward.

**3.** The axle moves hammers, which are used to crush stone.

## MAKE AND TEST A WATERWHEEL

**You will need:** two sturdy paper plates, eight disposable drink cups, adhesive tape, a pair of scissors, twine, a weight (for example, a small toy), a straw, string, two stakes, a bucket of water, an adult helper

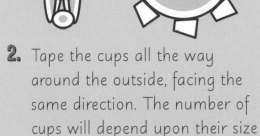

**1.** Tape the two paper plates together back-to-back, by running the adhesive tape all the way around the bottom of the plates. With an adult's help, punch a hole through the center of the plates using a pencil.

**2.** Tape the cups all the way around the outside, facing the same direction. The number of cups will depend upon their size and the size of the plates.

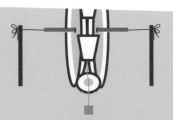

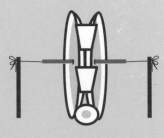

**3.** Push the straw through the center of the plates, and then thread some string through the straw. Tie the waterwheel onto stakes so that it is about chest height.

**4.** Tie a length of twine to a small weight and then tape it to the plates, between two of the cups.

**Once you have successfully raised the weight with your waterwheel, place your sticker here.**

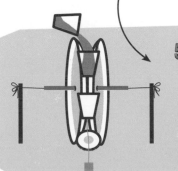

**5.** Start pouring water from the bucket into the cups. (It may be best to do this outside.) As the cups fill, the plates turn, and the weight rises.

**PLACE STICKER HERE**

⊘ TASK COMPLETE ⊘

# WIND AND WATER POWER TODAY

We are still capturing the power of wind and water today, but instead of grinding grain, windmills have been turned into huge turbines to make electricity. More and more "wind farms" are being built on land and out at sea. Hydroelectric power stations harness the movement of water to make electricity, mainly using dams and rivers. Like wind, water is a free source of energy that never runs out.

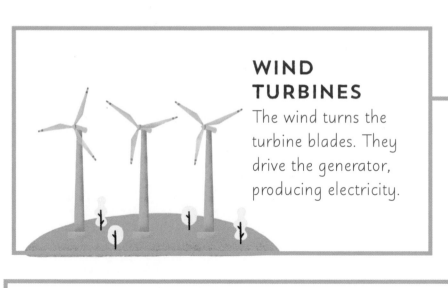

## WIND TURBINES

The wind turns the turbine blades. They drive the generator, producing electricity.

## HYDROELECTRIC POWER STATION

These are usually built in hilly places so they can use fast-flowing falling water. The water is collected in a dam and then allowed to flow downhill to spin turbine blades. The turbine powers a generator, which makes electricity.

## WAVE POWER STATIONS

The up-and-down movement of floating machines is converted into electricity. Sea covers two-thirds of the planet, so it could be a big source of energy, but it is difficult to capture its power. This means wave power stations are still quite rare.

## POWER LINES

The electricity made by wind turbines, hydroelectric power stations and wave power stations flows through power cables to homes, schools, factories and anywhere else it is needed.

ENGINEER INFO

# THE SUN

The sun sends us far more energy than is produced by all the world's power stations put together, so engineers and scientists are working on ways to capture it. This huge ball of fire gets so hot it is able to create energy through a process called nuclear fusion. This energy travels to Earth in the form of rays and is called radiation. Solar panels on rooftops take the energy in the sun's rays and convert it into electricity.

## TEST WHY SOLAR PANELS ARE ALWAYS DARK

**You will be leaving two ice cubes in the sun—one on a piece of black cardboard and another on a piece of white cardboard—and seeing which one melts quickest.**

**You will need:** black cardboard and white cardboard, two ice cubes, a sunny day

The ice cube on the black cardboard should melt first. This is because black is much better at absorbing the sun's energy.

**PLACE STICKER HERE**

**Once you have completed your experiment, place your sticker here.**

⟋ **TASK COMPLETE** ⟋

**CONGRATULATIONS!** You have now qualified as an
alternative energy engineer. Fill in the details on the certificate below.

# QUALIFIED ALTERNATIVE
# ENERGY ENGINEER

**ENGINEER NAME:**

The above-named engineer has
learned about wind, water and solar energy
and is now fully qualified in

## ALTERNATIVE ENERGY
## ENGINEERING.

**QUALIFICATION DATE:**

# MATERIALS ENGINEER

# PROPERTIES

Materials engineers work with metals, plastic and other materials. They design new materials and then test them to see how useful they are. The materials they work with have different properties, which makes them useful for different tasks. For example, you wouldn't make a window out of steel, or a ship out of wool. No property is better than another. It is all about finding the right material for the right task.

This list of 16 common properties has been split into pairs of opposites.

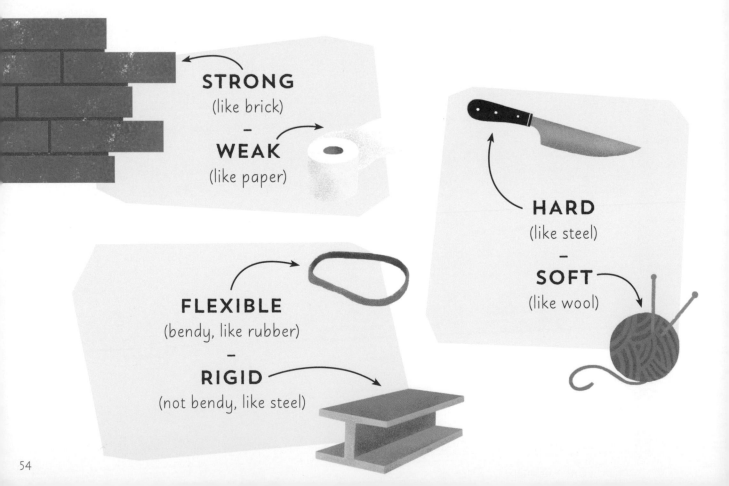

**STRONG**
(like brick)
-
**WEAK**
(like paper)

**HARD**
(like steel)
-
**SOFT**
(like wool)

**FLEXIBLE**
(bendy, like rubber)
-
**RIGID**
(not bendy, like steel)

## HEAVY
(like a lead weight)

–

## LIGHT
(like a feather)

## SMOOTH
(like a marble)

–

## ROUGH
(like sandpaper)

## TRANSPARENT
(something you can see through, like glass)

–

## OPAQUE
(something you can't see through, like wood)

## CONDUCTOR
(a conductor allows electricity or heat to flow through; copper is good for both of these.)

–

## INSULATOR
(does not allow electricity through, like the plastic that covers wires; or does not allow heat through, like wool)

## WATERPROOF
(keeps water out, like plastic or rubber)

–

## ABSORBENT
(soaks up water, like tissue paper, fabric or a sponge)

**i**

**ENGINEER INFO**

55

# STRENGTH: MAGIC METALS

Metals can have great strength. However, they can be strong in different ways and this gives them different uses.

**STEEL** is an alloy, which means it is a "mixed metal." It is mostly made from iron, but iron on its own is brittle (breaks easily) and rusts quickly, so another metal or substance is added. Steel can withstand a lot of pressure before it weakens or bends out of shape. It is also cheap to produce, so it is ideal for buildings. The huge metal frames that hold up skyscrapers are made of steel.

**ALUMINUM** is only about one-third as heavy as steel but is still strong for its weight. This makes it the perfect metal for making airplanes. Some bicycles are made from aluminum because a lighter bike is easier to pedal. Cans for drinks are often made out of aluminum because it doesn't rust and is light to transport.

**TUNGSTEN** keeps its strength at high temperatures and has an extremely high melting point (6,191°F). This makes it very useful where there are high temperatures, anywhere from the lightbulb in your home to rocket engine parts. It is also an extremely hard metal—about five times harder than steel—so it is used for making tools, such as drills and saws.

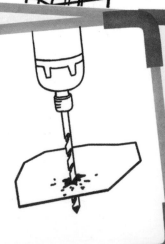

# INVESTIGATE THE STRENGTH OF DIFFERENT MATERIALS

**Different materials have different strengths. One way to measure a material's strength is to see if it is undamaged and the same shape when different forces are applied to it. You will be using different forces on different materials to see what happens.**

1. Put an X in each box below where you think the force will break or permanently change the shape. For example, if you think you can tear a piece of paper, put an X in that box.

2. When you have filled in the table, collect your materials and test each one with the five forces. How many of your predictions were correct?

FORCE

| MATERIAL | TEARING | STRETCHING | SQUASHING | SNAPPING | BENDING |
|---|---|---|---|---|---|
| **PAPER** (LETTER-SIZE) | | | | | |
| **WOOD** (ICE CREAM STICK) | | | | | |
| **METAL** (KEY) | | | | | |
| **PLASTIC** (SOFT DRINK BOTTLE) | | | | | |
| **RUBBER** (AN ERASER) | | | | | |

When you have completed the strength tests, place your sticker here.

**PLACE STICKER HERE**

⌀ TASK COMPLETE ⌀

# A TOWER OF
# STRENGTH

On the previous page, you looked at how different materials have different strengths. Design also plays an important part in making structures strong and stable. You can prove this by building towers out of…paper!

## DESIGN AND BUILD PAPER TOWERS

**You will be experimenting with three different designs. There are some examples shown here, but you can also create your own designs. See how high you can make your towers. The important thing is that they stand up on their own without you holding them!**

**You will need:** plenty of thick letter-size pieces of paper, adhesive tape, a pair of scissors, a tape measure

**1.** First, make some "struts" to hold up your towers. To make a strut, roll a piece of paper into a cylinder and tape it at the top, center and bottom. You can roll the paper up tightly to make the strut thin and strong, or roll it loosely to make the strut thicker and more steady.

**2.** Once you have plenty of struts, you can begin to assemble your towers. Make the floors of your towers by balancing flat pieces of paper on top of the struts. You can use adhesive tape to attach struts to each other.

**3.** When each tower is complete, use a tape measure to measure them and record the results in the table below. Which tower was the tallest?

|  | TOWER 1 | TOWER 2 | TOWER 3 |
|---|---|---|---|
| HEIGHT (INCHES) |  |  |  |

When you have built your towers, place your sticker here.

PLACE STICKER HERE

TASK COMPLETE

# FRICTION

If you stop pedaling when you are cycling, your bicycle will slow down and then stop. This is because of a force called friction. Friction acts between two surfaces that are rubbing together—in the case of your bike, that's the wheels and the ground. It is a force that slows objects down.

Different surfaces have different amounts of friction. This is why you can slide on smooth ice, which has little friction, but not on rough grass. Even air causes friction, which is why airplanes are designed with a narrow shape to reduce air resistance.

Sometimes, engineers change the amount of frictional force. For example, certain parts of a car are designed to increase friction, while other parts are designed to lower it.

* The tread (grip) on tires **INCREASES FRICTION** to stop cars from skidding on the road.

* The oil used in car engines **REDUCES FRICTION** by making surfaces that touch each other more slippery. Without oil, the friction of the fast-moving engine parts could create enough heat to damage the engine.

# TEST THE FRICTION OF DIFFERENT SURFACES

**You will need:** a marker to use as a starting point (for example, a pencil), something with wheels (a toy car is ideal), a tape measure

1. Push the toy car from the starting point as hard as you can across each of the following surfaces: carpet, wood, concrete and tile. (You can use different surfaces if you don't have these ones in your home.) Try to push the car with the same force each time. One way to do this is to lay your hand flat and flick the car with your thumb and index finger.

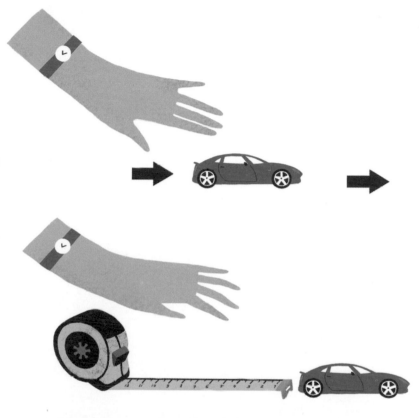

2. Measure how far the car moves from the starting point on each surface, and record your results in the table below.

|  | CARPET | WOOD | CONCRETE | TILES |
|---|---|---|---|---|
| **DISTANCE (INCHES)** |  |  |  |  |

**When you have recorded your results, place your sticker here.**

**PLACE STICKER HERE**

⊘ **TASK COMPLETE** ⊘

**CONGRATULATIONS!** You have now qualified
as a materials engineer. Fill in the details on the certificate below.

# — QUALIFIED —
# MATERIALS ENGINEER

**ENGINEER NAME:**

The above-named engineer
has learned about friction
and the properties of materials
and is now fully qualified in

## MATERIALS ENGINEERING.

**QUALIFICATION DATE:**

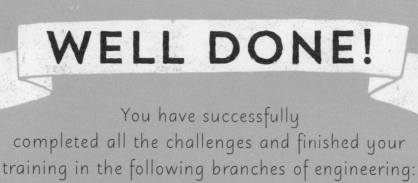

# WELL DONE!

You have successfully
completed all the challenges and finished your
training in the following branches of engineering:

**MECHANICAL, AEROSPACE, ROBOTICS,
ENERGY, ALTERNATIVE ENERGY, MATERIALS**

You are now ready to graduate from
Engineer Academy.

**AS PART OF YOUR GRADUATION CEREMONY,
YOU SHOULD READ THE ENGINEER'S CODE BELOW
AND PROMISE TO FOLLOW IT.**

Once you have done this, you can collect your
final qualification.

**1.** When carrying out my work, I will always
work safely and keep myself and other
people free from harm.

**2.** Before carrying out any work, I will always
check to make sure I understand what needs
to be done.

**3.** After completing a design, build or repair,
I will always carry out checks to make sure
the job has been done properly.

**4.** I understand that new inventions are
happening all the time and I will work
hard to keep my knowledge up to date.

Draw or glue
a picture of your
face here.

Signed:

- - - - - - - - - - - - - - - - - - - - - -

# ENGINEER'S TOOLBOX

- Pull-out game and press-out game cards, counters and die
- Poster
- Model (on the flaps of the book)
- Stickers

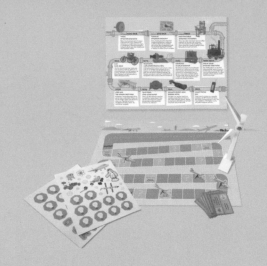

## RUNWAY RACE GAME INSTRUCTIONS

You'll find this game board on the reverse side of the pull-out poster. It is for two to four players. Push out the die, then fold and glue it. Push out the counters and the counter stands, then slot together. Each player needs one counter.

**Be the first plane to take off at the airport! Take turns to roll the die and see how many spaces to move. If you land on a blue square, pick a card and follow the directions. If you land on a square with wrenches, roll the required number on your turn to continue. The first player to reach the finish line and take off is the winner.**

## ANSWERS

**PAGE 35—learn about the dangers of electricity:**
1. There is a vase of flowers on the TV (liquid and electricity need to be kept apart); 2. There is a cloth on the lamp (this could cause a fire); 3. Wires are trailing across the floor (someone could trip on them); 4. There is a frayed wire; 5. The baby is sticking a spoon into the outlet; 6. The boy is poking something into the games console when it is plugged in (he could electrocute himself).

## PAGE 43

# RUNWAY RACE CARDS

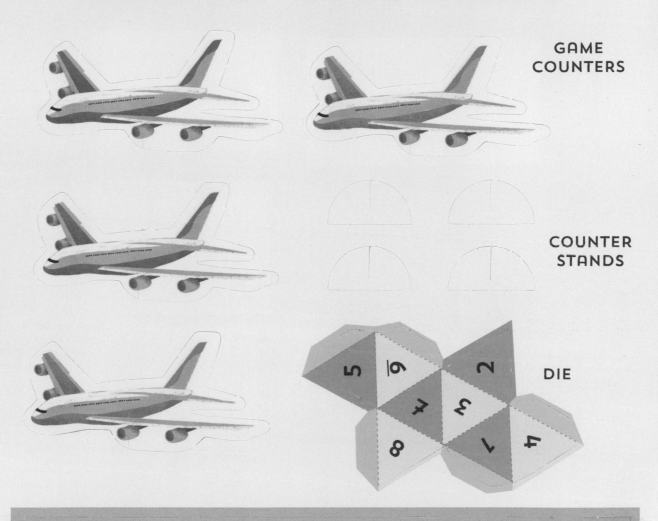

GAME COUNTERS

COUNTER STANDS

DIE

YOU'RE RIGHT ON TIME.
MOVE FORWARD ONE SPACE.

PLAYERS MUST CALL YOU CAPTAIN UNTIL THE GAME ENDS.

OH NO! SOME LUGGAGE HAS FALLEN OUT.
MOVE BACK TWO SPACES.

RUNWAY RACE

RUNWAY RACE

RUNWAY RACE

**YOUR PILOT HAS BOARDED.**

MOVE ALL OTHER PLAYERS BACK THREE SPACES.

---

**YOU'RE AHEAD OF SCHEDULE.**

MOVE FORWARD TWO SPACES.

---

**YOUR CABIN CREW AREN'T ON BOARD YET.**

MOVE BACK TWO SPACES.

---

**FOR ONE MINUTE, WALK AROUND THE ROOM WITH YOUR ARMS OUTSTRETCHED LIKE A PLANE.**

---

**YOUR ENGINE HAS A SERIOUS FAULT.**

GO BACK TO THE START.

---

**THE CONTROL TOWER HAS GIVEN YOU PERMISSION TO FLY.**

MOVE FORWARD THREE SPACES.

---

RUNWAY
RACE
RUNWAY
RACE
RUNWAY
RACE
RUNWAY
RACE
RUNWAY
RACE
RUNWAY
RACE

YOUR WHEELS ARE SQUEAKY.

MOVE BACK THREE SPACES.

MAKE A NOISE LIKE A PLANE FOR ONE MINUTE.

YOU ARE RUNNING LATE.

MOVE BACK ONE SPACE.

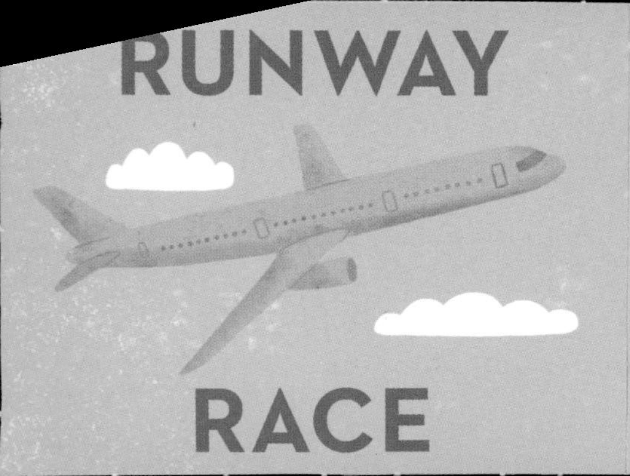
RUNWAY
RACE
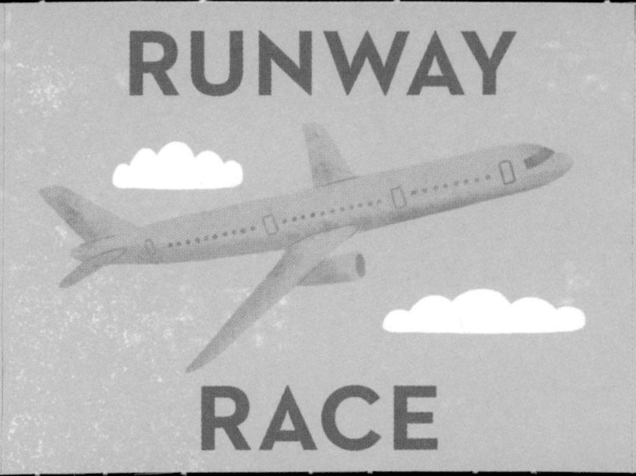
RUNWAY
RACE
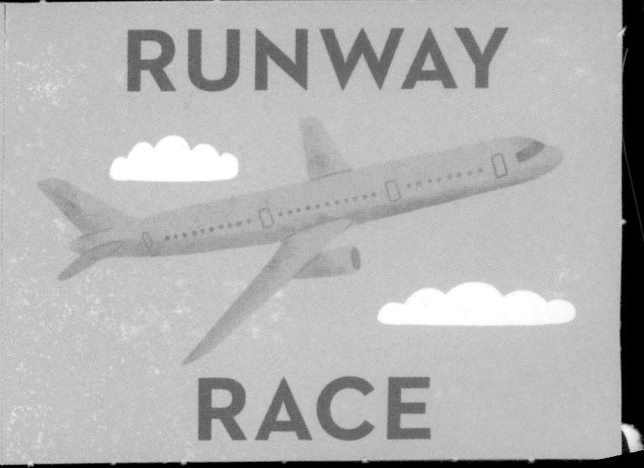
RUNWAY
RACE

## TELEPHONE

### ALEXANDER GRAHAM BELL

Although several inventors were tryin a device for sending voice messages distance, it was Alexander Graham B 1876, sent the famous telephone mes. Watson, come here; I want you." Grah. recognized as the inventor of the first

## CAR

### KARL BENZ

The first car only had three wheels and a top speed of 10 mph, but it revolutionized the world of transportation. Its inventor, Karl Benz, founded the Benz Motor Company and Mercedes-Benz is still producing cars today.

**1903**

**1925**

## TELEVISION

### JOHN LOGIE BAIRD

John Logie Baird demonstrated his new invention in a London shop in 1925 and five years later, his company started mass-producing his device, the "televisor."

## AIRPLANE

### THE WRIGHT BROTHERS

People have always dreamed of flying and in 1903, two brothers, Wilbur and Orville Wright, finally made the dream come true. They flew 120 feet in the "Kitty Hawk," the world's first airplane.

FINISH

PASSENGER
BOARDING

ROLL A 6
TO CONTINUE

WHEEL CHECK

**ROLL A 5
TO CONTINUE**

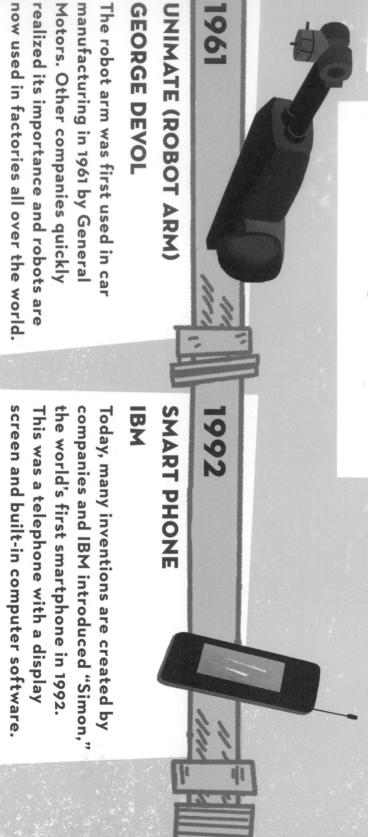

## COMPUTER
## CHARLES BABBAGE

The Difference Engine was an automatic calculator or, in other words, the world's first computer! Unfortunately, it needed 25,000 parts and would have been as big as a room, so the complete machine was never built. After ten years of work, a smaller version was produced, which proved that the design worked.

## STEAM TRAIN
## RICHARD TREVITHICK

The "Puffing Devil" was the first steam-powered vehicle. It made its first journey on December 24th, 1801. Just over two years later, Trevithick devised a vehicle that ran on rails—the first ever train!

---

g to create across a ell who, in sage: "Mr. am Bell was telephone.

---

## 1961

## UNIMATE (ROBOT ARM)
## GEORGE DEVOL

The robot arm was first used in car manufacturing in 1961 by General Motors. Other companies quickly realized its importance and robots are now used in factories all over the world.

---

## 1992

## SMART PHONE
## IBM

Today, many inventions are created by companies and IBM introduced "Simon," the world's first smartphone in 1992. This was a telephone with a display screen and built-in computer software.

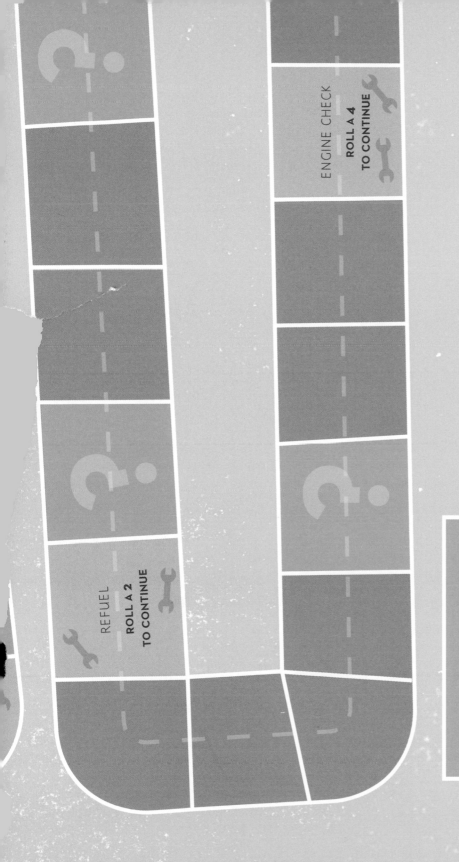

ENGINE CHECK
**ROLL A 4
TO CONTINUE**

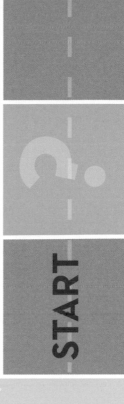

REFUEL
**ROLL A 2
TO CONTINUE**

START

PLACE YOUR
**RUNWAY
RACE CARDS**
HERE

# GREAT INVENTIONS

## At least 3500 BCE

### WHEEL

### INVENTOR UNKNOWN

One of the most important inventions of all time is the wheel. Without this invention, we wouldn't have cars, trains or even bicycles. Although essential for transportation, wheels may have initially been used to make pottery.

## Around 200 BCE

### COMPASS

### INVENTOR UNKNOWN

It was first discovered in C[...] a magnetized lodestone co[...] northward. But it was not u[...] 13th century that a magnet[...] was placed on top of a pin [...] a compass for sailors to use[...]

76

1885

**N**

hina that
uld point
ntil the
ized needle
o create
e to navigate.

**1822**

**1801-1804**

Around **1400**

### PRINTING PRESS
### JOHANNES GUTENBERG

There was a time when books were incredibly expensive because they had to be made by hand. The invention of the printing press meant that books could be produced in greater quantities at a much lower cost.

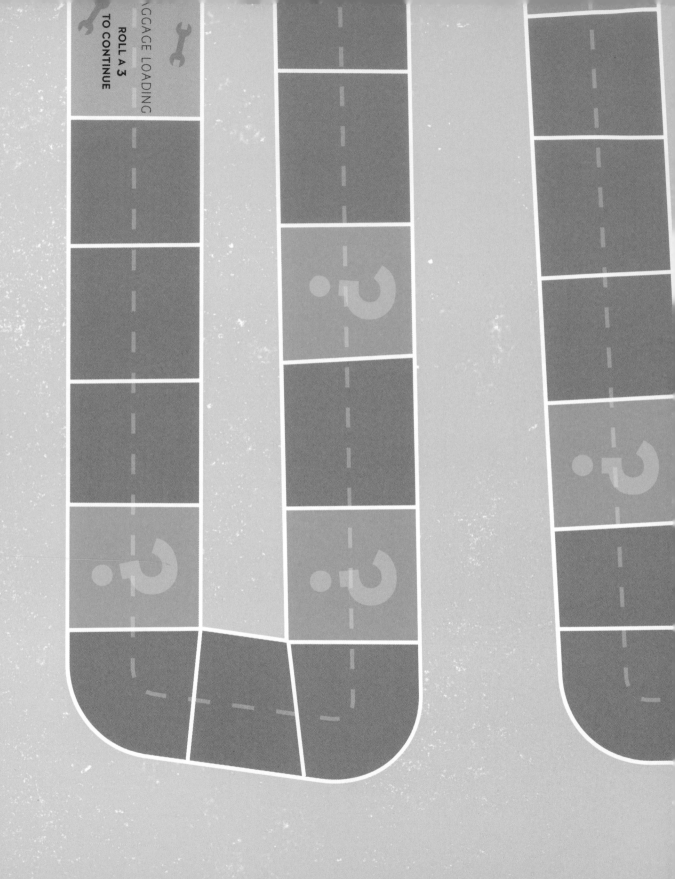

BAGGAGE LOADING

ROLL A 3
TO CONTINUE